OVERLEAF, PL. 1. *Self-portrait*. 20 x 12. 1939. Collection Hans and Helen Moller.

JOSEPH SOLMAN

INTRODUCTION BY

THEODORE F. WOLFF

Essays and Comments by

DORE ASHTON

SUZANNE BURREY

LAWRENCE CAMPBELL

A. L. CHANIN

SIDNEY JANIS

JO ANN LEWIS

STUART PRESTON

JOHN SIMON

NANCY STAPEN

HOWARD E. WOODEN

DA CAPO PRESS · NEW YORK

Library of Congress Cataloging-in-Publication Data

Joseph Solman / introduction by Theodore F. Wolff; essays and
   comments by Dore Ashton . . . [et al.].
      p.   cm.
      Includes bibliographical references.
      ISBN 0-306-79665-1 (hardcover: alk. paper). — ISBN 0-306-80639-8
   (paper : alk. paper)
      1. Solman, Joseph, 1909-   —Criticism and interpretation.
      I. Ashton, Dore.
ND237.S6327J67   1995
759.13—dc20
                                                  95–18606
                                                    CIP

Grateful acknowledgment is hereby given for permission
to reprint the following comments in this book:
Page 26, *Art in America*; page 84, *The New York Times*; page 118, *Arts Magazine*;
page 158, *The Washington Post*; page 173, *The Boston Globe*

The color photographs were made by Beckett Logan and Clive Russ

Published by Da Capo Press, Inc.
A Subsidiary of Plenum Publishing Corporation
233 Spring Street, New York, N.Y. 10013

EDITED AND DESIGNED BY ABE LERNER

PRINTED IN THE UNITED STATES OF AMERICA BY THE STINEHOUR PRESS

Contents

Introduction

BY THEODORE F. WOLFF

Joseph Solman is an art-world paradox. On the one hand, he is a "painter's painter," a "natural" with brush and pen who fought the good fight for modernism in his youth alongside such other stalwarts as Mark Rothko and Adolph Gottlieb, and who remains, six decades later, as passionately committed to that vision as ever.

On the other hand, his paintings, drawings and prints are admired by a remarkably broad spectrum of art lovers, as well as by both abstract and traditional painters.

There is a warmth and accessibility to Solman's art that belies its profound integrity, formal sophistication, and art-historical importance.

Solman's qualities as a painter were already very much in evidence as far back as the 1930s when, as a youngster still in his mid-twenties, he first brought them together in canvases of New York City street scenes and interiors that not only defined his creative vision, but helped carve a unique niche for himself in the annals of mid-twentieth century American art.

From the very beginning, drawing ranked high on his list of talents, as did his way with color and his ability to distill the character and mood of a place or an object into a handful of sensitively shaped and organized forms and colors. Particularly noteworthy—especially in one so young—was his grasp of the totality of his subjects and their "wholeness." He was able to translate that holistic perception into beautifully composed, richly evocative images that captured the pictorial essentials of a locale and tantalized the aesthetic sensibilities of those who viewed them.

Most of this came about naturally—supported by hard work and the sustained sharpening of his skills. But a significant portion of it resulted from a careful study of the artists he admired most.

Topping *that* list were Rembrandt, Cézanne, Daumier, Ryder, Rouault, and the early Matisse. All left their mark on him in one way or another. In some cases (Daumier, Ryder, Rouault), quite directly. In others, more obliquely, and generally in ways that focused at least as much on what it meant to be an artist as on how to achieve maximum effectiveness and significance as a painter.

But while Solman looked and learned, he neither imitated his heroes' work nor followed their examples blindly. He learned more about drawing while observing and sketching his fellow passengers on the subway travelling to the National Academy of Design than at the school itself. In this and in every other way, he remained very much his own man—a trait that would lead to dramatic and far-reaching consequences in a few years.

Solman's independence and interest in art manifested themselves while he was still very young. Born 1909 in Vitebsk, Russia, he migrated with his family to America in 1912, settling in Jamaica, Long Island. His mother would state in later years that he was already drawing at the crawling stage. His prowess with the pencil soon set him apart from most children his age. Indeed, his love of drawing left no doubt as to his future. "There was no question in my mind by the age of thirteen that I was going to be a painter," he told an interviewer in mid-career.

Determined to master the skills necessary to realize his goal, Solman enrolled at the National Academy of Design in 1926. He soon found its ultra-conservative climate inhospitable, and he left to study on his own. It wasn't easy, but once he found a studio in which to work, he managed to support himself by taking a succession of night jobs. That left him free to paint during the day and, just as important, to roam New York's art-filled galleries and museums in search of guidance and inspiration.

It was there, most particularly in the Metropolitan Museum of Art, and after it opened in 1929, the Museum of Modern Art, that he received his most valuable art education.

The time spent studying the modern masters soon bore fruit. By 1931 he was hard at work on a series of small gouaches of streets, alleys and railroad yards that incorporated lessons learned from Cubism, Klee and Rouault. A dozen of these were displayed the following year to good effect in the second Washington Square show. Also in 1932 Solman's work was accepted in the well-known Village Jumble Shop, juried by Reginald Marsh and Guy Pene Du Bois. Several were sold, and in 1934 he was given his first one-man show at the Contemporary Arts Gallery. This gallery also introduced the work of Mark Tobey, Rothko, and John Kane.

In a modest sense, Solman was on his way—especially since a leading newspaper art critic of the time wrote that his paintings were "marked by a genuine feeling . . . shot through with smouldering color, vague and haunting."

All this did not pay the rent, however. With the Depression well under way, Solman and his wife—he had married Ruth Romanofsky, a journalism student at N.Y.U. in 1933—were only too happy to accept the $21.50 a week the federal government's W.P.A. was paying artists for joining its Art Project.

Solman's involvement with the W.P.A. lasted until 1941. When it ended, he was no longer the promising but still rather raw young painter he had been when he had signed up in 1935.

A great deal had happened in those six years. There was a second, well-received one-man show; membership in the newly-formed Secession Gallery; and an invitation in 1938, from renowned art dealer J. B. Neumann to join his prestigious New Art Circle. Here Solman's paintings hung alongside canvases by such modern masters as Klee, Beckmann, and Rouault.

Before these events occurred, however, something even more important had taken place, both for Solman and for American art in general.

To understand its significance, one must step back a bit for an overview of American art between the two World Wars. Simply put, it was confused and lacking in direction. At one extreme were the Midwest Regionalist and American Scene painters led by Thomas Hart Benton and Grant Wood, who advocated a strictly grass roots American school of painting that owed as little as possible to the art of the past—and nothing at all to European modernism. At the other extreme were groups of modernists totally opposed to any form of parochial American art and passionately committed to the abstract and non-objective vision of European modernism. Several of the most militant of these banded together to form the American Abstract Artists, a clearly defined and effective organization that did much to disseminate some of modernism's more rarified formal theories to America as a whole. Arrayed in between these extremes, were other groups of various-minded artists. Some were clustered around charismatic leaders such as Stuart Davis, Arshile Gorky, and Willem de Kooning, while others worked independently but met regularly to argue art and theory. Still others painted in near total isolation, waiting for their time to come.

In 1935 another group came into being. Known as The Ten, it advocated a more diverse approach for an art that combined "a social consciousness with an abstract expressionistic heritage, thus saving art from merely propaganda on the one hand, or mere formalism on the other." Its original members were Ben-Zion, Ilya Bolotowsky, Adolph Gottlieb, Louis Harris, Jacob Kufeld, Mark Rothko, Louis Schanker, Nahum Tchacbasov and Joseph Solman.

For Solman, helping organize The Ten was a major event. He went on to become one of its most effective members, placing himself at the cutting edge of American art. He was also responsible for the designing of The Ten's announcements, whose modern, cryptic style, unique in the mid 1930s, may have set the showcard fashion now quite common.

With the formation of The Ten, painting in the United States would never again be quite the same. During its five years' existence its members would not only, in Solman's words, "give each other heart for a valuable period of time" but they would mature and toughen as creative figures and, in a number of cases, go on to significantly influence the course of American art for the next several decades.

From the start, The Ten provoked controversy. "These young artists are completely un-inhibited," art critic Henry McBride declared. "They attack a canvas with as much fury and excitement as they would spend attacking a government. . . . They dare any theme, and in a splashing, dashing, youthful fashion get away with it." Among the most daring was Solman. More importantly, he was one of the very best.

This has not always been sufficiently recognized by most art historians whose primary focus has been on the two most famous painters to emerge from the group: Mark Rothko and Adolph Gottlieb.

The Ten, in fact, has all too often been seen as little more than a breeding ground for ideas and attitudes that fed into and helped shape the nature and course of Abstract Expressionism a decade later. It completely ignores a factor of equal importance: the quality of the work produced by members of The Ten during the five years of its existence.

That it was high is beyond dispute. Solman, Rothko, Gottlieb, Bolotowsky, Ben-Zion, Graham and Kerkam have all been accorded major museum retrospectives. The paintings that have survived hold their own as serious and significant works of art.

And if that is true of anyone's canvases, it is particularly true of Solman's. Howard Da Lee Spencer, curator of the Wichita Art Museum's major 1984 Solman exhibition, put it this way: "During the 1930s Solman produced works which were among the most abstract and innovative paintings created by any member of The Ten . . . Solman synthesized analytical abstraction with expressionistic abstraction with the result that each of his works has a uniquely vibrant and animate feeling . . . He avoided themes of social protest or the urban decay of the Social Realists, and instead kept his art pure, non-topical, and on a level above the restraints of subject . . . As a result his paintings . . . have a fresh, universal, and undated appeal which seems as much a part of our own time as the time they were painted about five decades ago."

Much of this stems from his early maturity as a painter. The basic elements of his art were already firmly in place while he was still in his mid-twenties. The subtle subsequent changes that occurred in his work occurred organically and logically from within, and not as the result of external pressures, either economic or professional.

When The Ten disbanded in 1940, Solman, at the age of thirty-one, was an accomplished

artist, with a number of his finest paintings completed. He would in the following decades produce works of wider range and subtlety. He would also become a first-rate portraitist, produce outstanding monotypes, and continue to improve as a draftsman. But he would never alter his basic vision nor change the direction of his art. In that he was adamant.

Not every member of The Ten felt that way. Bolotowsky, for instance, quickly turned to pure abstraction. Gottlieb moved toward a highly personal ideographic imagery. And Rothko, eventually the most famous of all, gradually banished any semblance of representationalism from his work in order ultimately to fashion an art of almost pure color.

Solman, however, held firm, and by doing so, left us with one of the most intriguing questions pertaining to the art of that period: Why didn't he, with so much talent and skill at his disposal, participate in the formation of the New York School/Abstract Expressionist movement that was attracting a number of his colleagues, and that would, in a few short years, bring fame and glory to Rothko, Gottlieb, Jackson Pollock and a handful of others?

The obvious answer is: creative integrity. But true as that may be, it still does not totally clarify the issue. From all indications, neither Rothko nor Gottlieb, nor any of the other major figures of the New York School, "sold out" or compromised their ideals for immediate gain. Quite the opposite. For each of them the highly risky process that led from relatively conservative beginnings to front-line art-world activism as members of the international avant-garde, was both logical and appropriate. Not so with Solman, however, and therein lies much of what is special and significant about the artist and the man.

I put the question to him myself, and his response was immediate: "There were still too many aspects of the universe I wanted to paint." He has also said that nothing in his imagination can match what he sees in nature. And then there's his credo, which spells it out clearly and precisely: "I like the direct, even blunt, portrayal of my subject. Otherwise, I adhere to ancient rules: composition, lucid drawing, and color harmony—hoping to guide and control nature into an arresting design."

For Solman, art is an act of exploration and discovery, an intense painterly dialogue between the appearance of a subject and its most provocatively satisfying pictorial potential. He addresses nature as a respectful equal, determined to translate its varied effects on him into images capable of invoking similar feelings in others. As such, he wants to shape and share, not to preach or propound.

Given these objectives, how could any artist so inclined be satisfied with a slavish imitation of the appearance of nature, or more to the point of this discussion, give up so meaningful and dynamic a creative dialogue for another style of painting which, while possibly more "advanced" and professionally rewarding, embodied little of his unique vision and perceptions?

Obviously, no artist of passion and integrity could—or would. If anything, Solman is a shining example of an artist of outstanding abilities and accomplishments who has continued to grow in depth, subtlety and significance for six decades by remaining true to his vision, and by painting what he knows best in the best way he knows. And should that sound simplistic, it would be wise to remember that that was also the secret of Cézanne's impact and importance.

In this age of painters' excesses and fatuous simplifications, it is good to be reminded by someone like Solman that the best art isn't always the most extreme. That, indeed, artistic quality is often a matter of carefully achieved balance.

Nowhere is this demonstrated more clearly in Solman's work than in his portraits. To study them individually is to be impressed by his ability to translate physical characteristics and personality into paint. To view them collectively is to be even more impressed by the extraordinary range of painterly and formal devices at his command. Every portrait bears the stamp of his highly personal approach, yet no two are alike.

In Solman's hands, portraiture becomes a remarkable act of perceptual and psychological distillation. He uncovers both what is unique about each sitter and how best to convey that quality to others. The results are startlingly direct "speaking likenesses" of real human beings in richly-hued canvases that exist as provocatively designed modern works of art.

This seamless fusion of the actual and the abstract, the real and the created, has always lain at the core of Solman's art. It is as apparent in his early urban scenes as it is in his middle period still-life *Autumn Leaves*, 1950, Pl.92, the 1959 portrait of *Walter Starkie*, Pl.128, and the recent *Hallway* of 1987, Pl.183. It invariably manifests itself as a perfect if somewhat precarious balance between nature respectfully observed and nature distorted for compositional or expressive effect. This dynamic, "on edge" quality is, of course, intentional, for Solman's paintings are never static, never at rest. They reverberate with an energy that ranges from the subtle and sensitively controlled *Studio*, 1950, Pl.82, to the restless and barely contained *Martin Dworkin*, 1983, Pl.175. In fact, many of his canvases pulsate with so much energy that one suspects it took all of his considerable formal skills to keep everything in order.

One way Solman exercises guidance and control is through color. In this he is unique. Unlike many painters who prefer to work within a narrow color range, Solman uses color freely and in whatever way he deems appropriate. This is especially true in his portraits, where color is used to underscore everything from physical idiosyncrasies to character and personality traits. Thus, in *Naomi*, 1951, Pl.115, an all-pervasive blue projects a fine reflective mood, while in *Chris*, 1969, Pl.164, loosely brushed washes of oranges, yellows, and pinks help define the gentle, introspective nature of the sitter.

It would be a mistake, however, to single out only one or another of Solman's attributes as a painter. His greatest talent lies in his ability to see things in their totality, and so orchestrate the various elements of his paintings that they fuse together into a seamlessly unified whole. *That* is his special attribute and the one that not only defines him as an artist, but that sets him apart from the majority of his colleagues as well.

Above all, Solman's art is both civilized and civilizing. It is the product of an exceptional artist's lifelong pursuit of harmony and order within the locale, culture and creative mode he knows and loves best. That he has succeeded in his pursuit is clearly evident—just as it is evident that he has always been, and that he remains—even into his eighties—a valued and highly respected member of the American art community.

Measurements of the paintings are given in inches, height first.
All are oil on canvas unless otherwise stated.
If the location of a work is not shown, it is in the possession of the artist.

Early Works, 1927–30

PL. 2. *Sid*. 17 x 14. 1927. Collection Ann Levine, San Francisco, California.

PL. 3. *Bootblack*. 8 x 6½. 1929.

PL. 4. *Parsons Boulevard*.
18 x 22. 1929.

PL. 5. *Meyer*. 19 x 15. 1930.

PL. 6. *Ruth*. 19 x 16½. 1931.

Exploration, 1931–33

PL. 7. *Railroad Yard, Jamaica*. Gouache. 7½ X 10. 1931.

PL. 8. *Abandoned Cars, South Jamaica*. Gouache. 7 X 10. Private Collection.

PL. 9. *Nocturne, East River*. 7½ X 10. 1931.

PL. 10. *Street in Brooklyn*. Gouache. 10 x 7½. 1932.

PL. 11. *Country Road*. Gouache. 10 x 7½. 1931.

PL. 12. *Blacksmith's Shop*. 22 x 34. 1932. Collection Bram and Sandra Dyjkstra.

Discovery, 1935

PL. 13. *Rooftop*. Oil on board. 16 x 24. 1935. Collection Laura and Jeffrey London.

PL. 14. *The Poet*. 32 X 24. 1935.

PL. 15. *Interior With Easel.* 20 X 12. 1935.

PL. 16. *Moonlight*. 24 x 18. 1935. Private Collection.

PL. 17. *Interior at Evening*. Oil on board. 16 x 24. 1935. Private Collection.

PL. 18. *Cat in Alleyway*. 32 x 16. 1935.

PL. 19. *Green Cat.* 24 X 16. 1935.

PL. 20. *Junk Shop*. Oil on board. 20 X 35. 1935.

New York Street Scenes, 1936–42

BY LAWRENCE CAMPBELL

In the days of the W.P.A. and the American Artists Union, when regionalist and social protest painting began to make its mark in America, a group of young avant-gardists met in Joseph Solman's New York studio to form The Ten. Founding members were Solman, Mark Rothko, Adolph Gottlieb, Illya Bolotowsky, Louis Schanker, Ben-Zion, Nahum Tschacbasov, Louis Harris and Jankel Kufeld, who were later joined by Ralph Rosenborg, Earl Kerkam and John Graham. The Ten represented two new trends in American art: Expressionism and Symbolism.

By 1936, the year both The Ten and the American Abstract Artists were founded, Solman's technique was already decisive. He took a number of new admirations—Matisse, Klee, de Chirico, Cézanne—and superimposed them over earlier models such as Luks, Myers, and Whistler. It is not necessary to hunt for his signature—usually tucked away in some obscure part of the painting—to recognize one of his pictures. Apart from the characteristically expressionist distortions—the black lines which contoured his forms and unified his compositions, the swelling of the spaces between the lines, the thickness of the paint, the medley of superbly patterned shapes, the moodily Luminist coloring—there was evident that respect for a two-dimensional surface which marks the truly modern painting. The brilliance and poetry of these early works could be appreciated anew in these two recent shows.

In his introduction to a book of poetry by the English Poet Laureate John Betjeman, W. H. Auden introduced the word "topophilia" to characterize a special kind of affection for place. Solman is a pure topophile. It was not, however, the vision of an urban—or rather, urbane—America which drew him so much as the small neighborhood streets and houses he visited day in and day out: a stop on the Third Avenue El was for Solman certainly more beautiful than the soaring Chrysler Building. Indeed, Solman's brand of topophilism would prefer a view of a leaking fire hydrant to a view of untrammeled nature. His eyes are open to empty lots, to playgrounds, to where the pencil of the sky touches the sidewalk on crosstown streets. Solman painted Klein's Department Store in *Union Square*, 1936; the huge eyeball opposite the El in *The Oculist*, 1937; the large hanging street sign of a standing female which he calls *Venus on 23rd Street*, 1937; and everywhere the expressive garbage cans (almost a trademark), fire hydrants, subway kiosks and cellar doors belonging to ice and coal street-merchants that made up the extraordinary Toonerville that is New York to him. (The oils were done from notes in his studio; the gouaches, outdoors, from direct observation.)

Stephen Vincent Benét wrote "American Names" but the reader of this poem, which finishes with the famous line "Bury my heart at Wounded Knee," is not convinced that the poet had ever been there. "Bury My Heart on Avenue B" would be what a true topophile like Solman would have written. For viewers who admire his later paintings, especially those of the '50s, these earlier works, filled with sentiment and mood, will be a revelation.

Art in America, May, 1983.

PL. 21. *Trunk and Garage*. 26 x 36. 1936. Collection Alfred Knobler.

PL. 22. *25th Street Armory, New York City*. 26 x 36. 1936. Collection Lehmann Brothers.

PL. 23. *Cellar with Horseshoe*. 20 X 24. 1936. Collection Mr. and Mrs. Duffy.

PL. 24. *Harbor.* 20 X 32. 1936. Collection Paul Solman.

PL. 25. *Theatre*. 26 x 36. 1936. Collection Mr. and Mrs. Goldstein.

PL. 26. *Martin Craig*. 20 X 12. 1936. Hirshhorn Museum, Washington, D.C.

PL. 27. *Union Square*. 26 x 36. Collection Mr. and Mrs. Max Margulis.

42nd Street Shuttle, 1937

BY HOWARD E. WOODEN

Beneath New York City's well known 42nd Street, one short section of subway operates to connect two of the main branches of the extensive New York subway system. The underground station there is dingy and drab and late at night it is almost entirely deserted. One wonders why such a subject would be chosen as the theme for a work of art. Yet it is the artist who has the unique capability of finding beauty and mystery in the most unexpected places. This explains why the American artist Joseph Solman executed this 1937 painting, *42nd Street Shuttle*.

What we see here is a view of the underground platform and an emergency train bumper with a red stop signal marking the end of the shuttle line. Nearby stand two men, one a subway workman and the other perhaps a passenger waiting for the shuttle to arrive. In the upper left is seen a passenger descending the stairs leading down from ground level.

In no sense, however, is this a literal representation of the underground, for the forms depicted—all heavily outlined in black—are expressively suggested rather than accurately described, thus allowing the viewer's imagination to come into play and complete the scene. Moreover, although such traditional spatial cues as receding lines and receding masses are clearly in evidence, Solman has intentionally distorted the overall space encompassed here by exaggerating the tilt of the platform floor as it extends into the distance, thereby charging the composition with a dynamic quality that echoes the nature of the setting itself.

But such energy derives even more from Solman's use of rich and boldly contrasting colors. Solman has always been a strong colorist and in this work, by means of color control and the use of modulated saturations of red, he has created a vibrant and lively space, totally independent of subject matter. And that sense of aliveness achieved by color usage is further intensified by the radiant glow emanating from many of the forms edged with a narrow fringe of green or turquoise blue.

What is especially significant about this work is that Solman has produced the equivalent of an abstract expressionist painting a full decade before the abstract expressionist movement came to dominate the American art scene, but without abandoning identifiable forms. At the same time, the strong flat geometric shapes appearing throughout the composition, and in particular such signs and emblems as the circular stop light and the arrow on the long diagonal red band, suggest features of what will later be assimilated as image-types used by Pop and Photo-Realist artists.

PL. 28. *42nd Street Shuttle*. 25 x 34. Wichita Art Museum. Wichita, Kansas.

PL. 29. *Sign Painting*. Gouache. 8 x 12. 1937. Collection Paul Solman.

PL. 30. *Cherchez La Femme*. 8 x 10. Collection Frank and Nettie Donnola.

PL. 31. *Surgical Store Window*. Gouache. 14 x 10. Wichita Art Museum.

PL. 32. *Garage*. 25 X 34. 1937. Collection Eva Roman Haller.

PL. 33. *The Violinist*. 32 X 24. 1937. Private Collection.

PL. 34. *Horse and Wagon.* 10 x 14. Collection Mr. and Mrs. Joe Miller.

PL. 35. *Coal Bin.* 28 x 38. 1937. Private Collection.

PL. 36. *Budapest String Quartet*. 16 x 24. 1937.

PL. 37. *West 23rd Street*. Gouache. 11 x 14. 1937.

PL. 38. *The Oculist*. 25 x 34. 1937. Collection Eva Roman Haller.

PL. 39. *Venus of 23rd Street*. 29 x 23. 1937. Collection Eva Roman Haller.

PL. 40. *Naomi*. 32 x 24. 1938.

PL. 41. *Park Sentinel.* 24 x 36. 1937.

PL. 42. *Avenue B.* 24 x 32. 1937. Collection Judy Solman.

PL. 43. *The Red Semaphore*. 26 x 36. 1937. Collection Mrs. V. Leventritt.

PL. 44. *Tenement Garden.* 25 X 34. 1938. Collection Mr. and Mrs. Joe Miller.

PL. 45. *Watching an Excavation.* 30 x 36. 1938. Private Collection.

PL. 46. *Clinton Corners, New York*. 26 x 36. 1938. Private Collection.

PL. 47. *Ice Cellar*. 26 x 36. 1937. Private Collection.

PL. 48. *Under the El.* 26 x 36. 1938. Collection Mr. and Mrs. Stan Schneider.

PL. 49. *Statue in Madison Square Park*. 36 x 26. 1938.

PL. 50. *Jefferson Tower*. 26 x 36. 1938. Collection Charlotte Golden.

PL. 51. *New York Nocturne*. 26 x 36. 1938. Collection Bram and Sandra Dyjkstra.

PL. 52. *Red Fire Escape*. 26 x 36. 1938. Collection Sandy and Jack Schwab.

PL. 53. *Junk Shop*. Watercolor. 4 x 5. 1938. Private Collection.

PL. 54. *Green Ice Cellar*. 28 x 38. 1938. Collection John Rushton.

PL. 55. *East Side Playground*. 30 x 38. 1937. Collection Paul Solman.

PL. 56. *Houseboat*. 20 X 32. 1936. Collection Annie Rogin.

PL. 57. *Tinsmith Shop*. 36 x 47. 1939–40. Private Collection.

PL. 58. *Madison Square Park*. 26 x 36. Collection Mr. and Mrs. William Sallar.

Loft Period, 1938–42

EARLY INTERIORS, STILL LIFES, PORTRAITS

BY SIDNEY JANIS

The still lifes, interiors and portrait studies included in the present exhibition [at the Bonestell Gallery, 1942] reflect moments of quiet inner serenity. Originally, vibrating exteriors came from the brush of Joseph Solman. Between these phases there is no sharp break for they are part of a cycle yet to be completed.

In the early period the spectator found himself traversing Solman's bold, expressionist Streets, and later, peering into his subtle, more abstract Ice Cellars. Now, he enters the painter's studio, where through obliquely opening windows, once again he sees the street. His viewpoint has been reversed, and with it, the lights and darks of all he gazes upon. The style as well has altered, being neither abstract nor expressionist but rather a fusion of the two.

Solman, in his studio interiors, pays homage to various masters of the past by including single examples of each in his compositions, either on the wall or on the table, and each gives the clue to the motif for Solman's immediate design. There is no eclecticism, nor is there any sacrifice of his own personal style, for this motif does not come from the master's iconography but is imaginatively formed by Solman himself. Always the sensitive colorist, his crisp, dry, spontaneous spreading of pigment is thoroughly worked into his plastic theme.

PL. 59. *Loft Interior*. Oil on board. 16 x 20. 1941. Collection Dorothy Margolin.

PL. 60. *Interior with Corot Print*. 20 X 12. 1941. Private Collection.

PL. 61. *Ruth with Pink Robe*. Oil on board. 20 X 12. 1938.

PL. 62. *Books and Ruler*. Oil on board. 12 X 20. 1940.

PL. 63. *Open Window*. Oil on board. 18 x 12¼. 1940.

PL. 64. *Blue Blotter*. Oil on board. 12 X 20. 1939.

PL. 65. *The Sewing Basket*. Oil on board. 12 X 20. 1940.

PL. 66. *Books*. 12 x 20. 1940. Collection Mr. and Mrs. Harry Kosovsky.

PL. 67. *Ben-Zion*. 24 x 30. 1939.

PL. 68. *Edmund Weil.* 30 x 20. 1940.

PL. 69. *Ruth Reading.* 26 x 36. 1939.

PL. 70. *Books and Cigar Box*. Oil on board. 16 x 20. 1941. Collection Wichita Art Museum.

PL. 71. *The Modern Museum Catalogue*. Oil on cotton. 18 x 18. 1940.

PL. 72. *Metaphysical Still Life*. 24 x 30. 1940.

PL. 73. *The Paintbox*. 18 x 24. 1940. Whereabouts Unknown.

PL. 74. *Self Portrait*. 24 x 18. 1941. National Academy of Design.

PL. 75. *Mother and Child*. Oil on board. 20 x 12. 1942.

PL. 76. *Ruth*. 24 x 20. 1941. Collection Rachel Solman.

PL. 77. *St. George Church, Grey Day*. Oil on board. 20 x 12. 1942. Collection Dr. and Mrs. Sam Prince.

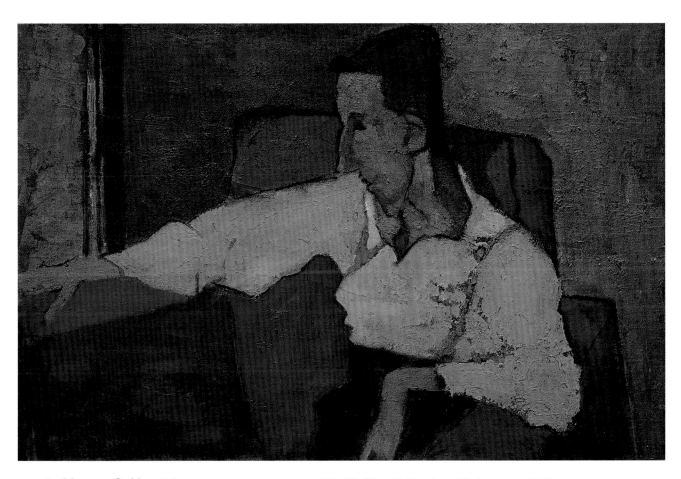

PL. 78. *Murray Golden*. Oil on cotton. 12 x 16. 1942. The Phillips Collection, Washington, D.C.

Studio Interiors, 1945–51

BY STUART PRESTON

INTIMIST: There is no suspicion of a formula in Joseph Solman's poetic paintings of studio interiors at the A.C.A. Gallery. For this intimist, the working of reflected light playing over the disorder of a room is the main thing. But light is not merely used to illustrate each rickety chair or abandoned easel; it is principally a means of forcing the spectator to discover strange beauties in unpromising places. A justifiable comparison with the approach of Vuillard can be made here. Solman's interest in the bare bones of a design lead him to certain formal distortions, deliberate awkwardnesses of drawing whose purpose is to give the forms happier breathing space within the design. There are numerous such subtleties and they are matched by the beautiful nuances of pale color which establish the tone of a given canvas and which are occasionally set off by startling passages of bright color, like the scarlet book in *Interior With Statue*. And if the delight of fine observation dominates these paintings, there is also a note of strangeness in the absence of all figures when everything speaks of human presence. It is by the distinguished portraits here, particularly by the pathos of *Eddie*, that Solman's responsiveness to character can be judged.

The New York Times, 1952.

Photo, corner of studio

PL. 79. *Window Interior*. Oil on board. 12 X 20. 1947. Collection Mr. and Mrs. Max Margulis.

PL. 80. *Solitude*. 12 x 20. 1947. Collection Mr. and Mrs. Larry Marks.

PL. 81. *The Broom*. Oil on board. 20 x 16. 1947. The Phillips Collection, Washington, D.C.

PL. 82. *The Studio*. Oil on board. 16 x 20. 1948. Rose Art Museum, Waltham, Massachusetts.

PL. 83. *The Matchbox*. Oil on board. 16 x 20. 1949. Collection Mr. and Mrs. Sidney Thomas.

PL. 84. *The El Greco Print*. Oil on board. 12 x 20. 1948. The Phillips Collection, Washington, D.C.

PL. 85. *Fragments of a Studio*. 20 x 24. 1949. Whereabouts Unknown.

PL. 86. *Open Windows*. 12 x 20. 1948. Collection Mary Weisstein.

PL. 87. *Studio Corner*. 20 X 12. 1950. Collection Caroline Goodman.

PL. 88. *Lying Figure*. Oil on board. 16 x 20. 1948. Whereabouts Unknown.

PL. 89. *Japanese Model*. 16 x 20. 1948. Collection Harold and Lucette White.

PL. 90. *Model Reading*. 12 x 6. 1948. Hirshhorn Museum, Washington, D.C.

PL. 91. *Nude*. Oil on board. 12 x 20. 1948. Collection Caroline Goodman.

PL. 92. *Autumn Leaves*. 16 x 24. 1950. Collection Mr. and Mrs. Joe Miller.

PL. 93. *Still Life*. Oil on board. 12 X 20. 1947. University of Arizona.

PL. 94. *Studio*. 24 X 30. 1951. Collection Dr. and Mrs. Sam Prince.

PL. 95. *The Red Pencil.* 16 x 20. 1948. Collection Hank and Carol Goldberg.

PL. 96. *The Purple Window*. 20 x 30. 1950. Private Collection.

PL. 97. *The Blue Book*. 24 x 16. 1950. Collection Dr. and Mrs. Alan Barry.

PL. 98. *Interior with Pink Cloth*. 18 x 24. 1950. Whitney Museum, New York.

PL. 99. *Study in Red and Green*. Oil on board. 12 x 20. 1950. Collection Mr. and Mrs. M. Vanderwoude.

PL. 100. *Elaine*. 36 x 24. 1950. Private Collection.

PL. 101. *Studio with Mexican Jug*. 36 x 30. 1951. Collection Abe Lerner.

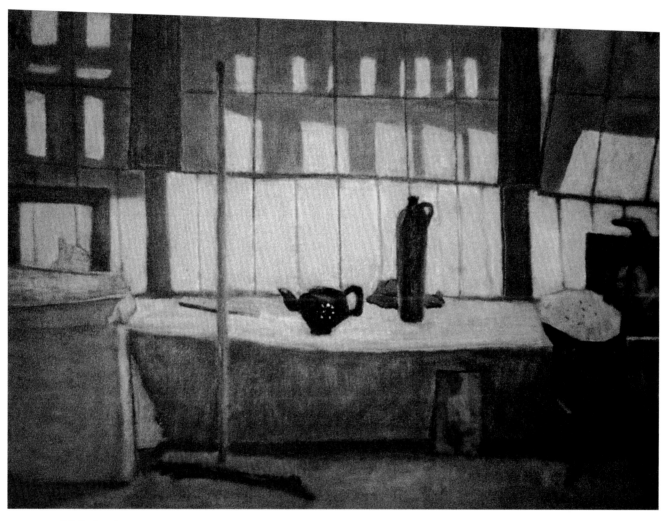

PL. 102. *Light in August*. 26 x 36. 1951. Private Collection.

PL. 103. *Cigar Box*. 18 x 24. 1950. Collection Dorothy Margolin.

PL. 104. *Statue*. 16 x 24. 1950. Hirshhorn Museum, Washington, D.C.

PL. 105. *Books and Teapot*. Oil on board. 12 x 20. 1951.

PL. 106. *Sculptor's Stand.* 24 x 16. 1951.

PL. 107. *Green Studio*. Oil on board. 16 x 24. 1949. Collection Ronni Solman.

PL. 108. *Blue Statuette*. 16 x 24. 1949. Private Collection.

PL. 109. *Studio*. 18 x 24. 1950. Collection Dr. Joseph Mandelbaum.

PL. 110. *Eddie*. 20 x 16. 1950. Private Collection.

PL. 111. *Regards From Chicago*. Oil on board. 16 x 20. 1948. Dayton Art Institute, Dayton, Ohio.

Some Doubting Thomases to the contrary it is quite possible to dispose paint in such a way as can only be described as magical.

The truth of this should be apparent to anyone with an eye for color and texture who examines several canvases which Joseph Solman is showing at Esther's Alley Gallery.

The Solman items referred to reveal cunningly arranged planes of neutral tones, set off by a touch or two of full-hued color. This sounds simple enough, yet it requires a world of skill and sensitivity to bring it off. The canvases present an extraordinary combination of the literal and abstract.

Herman Reuter. Hollywood Citizen-News, March 13, 1948.

PL. 112. *Chairs and Broom.* 28 x 50. 1951. Collection Paul Solman.

Transitions

BY SUZANNE BURREY

While Rothko and Gottlieb explored Greek myths and anthropology in search of universal symbols, Solman regarded his own studio—tables, chairs, books, pens, cigar boxes, drawings, even the reproductions of Corot and Matisse, which provided the leitmotif in some of his interior compositions—and painted a personal set of symbols, of a humble, household universality. It was a Chardin-like turning away from an academy of neo-classicism, hybrid with anthropology and abstraction in its contemporary American version. Except for the folio, *Twelve Studies for a Mozart Portrait*, Solman was occupied with studio interiors and still lifes for the next years. These, with some of the early street scenes, were shown at a retrospective at the Phillips Gallery, Washington, D. C., in 1949, Duncan Phillips himself having purchased several of his paintings. Then, after he had reached a certain point of fulfillment in painting the objects in his world, Solman was moved to paint its *dramatis personæ*.

From the article "Joseph Solman: The Growth Of Conviction" in *Arts Magazine*, October, 1955.

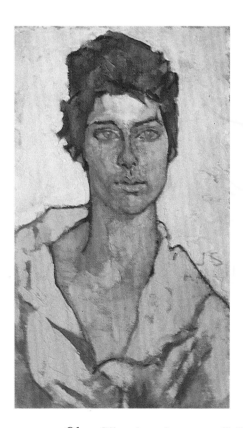

PL. 113. *Olga*. Oil on board. 20 x 12. Collection Olga Boikess.

PL. 114. *Rose Bank*. 36 x 28. 1950. Collection Stephen Bank.

PL. 115. *Naomi*. 20 x 16. 1951. Hirshhorn Museum, Washington, D.C.

PL. 116. *Ronni*. 30 X 24. 1950. Hirshhorn Museum, Washington, D.C.

PL. 117. *B. J. O'Neill.* 24 x 18. 1950. Whereabouts unknown.

PL. 118. *Byron Browne*. 36 x 26. 1954. Hirshhorn Museum, Washington, D.C.

PL. 119. *Paul.* 20 X 16. 1949.

PL. 120. *Lottie*. Oil on board. 20 x 12. 1954. Collection Lottie Altman.

PL. 121. *Natalie*. 36 x 28. 1960. Collection Bernard Braddon.

PL. 122. *Bernard.* 45 X 20. 1957. Collection Bernard Braddon.

PL. 123. *Marie.* 36 X 26. 1959.

PL. 124. Detail of Pl. 123.

The Sitter as Subject

BY DORE ASHTON

One of Joseph Solman's contemporaries, the painter Will Barnet, called him a painter's painter. By that he didn't mean that only a painter could fully respond to his work. Rather, that in Solman's work, the art of the painter was respected in every aspect, and that the painterly conventions of some five hundred years of art history had been studied, absorbed and refreshed in one painter's contribution to its flow. This is not a matter of traditionalism. It is a matter of métier. All good painters love their materials and their means, struggling lifetimes to refine and enliven them.

Although Solman has made accomplished paintings in several genres, I have admired above all his portraits—a genre he stubbornly developed in spite of its languishing status in the United States during the years Solman entered his professional life. Solman, whose fundamental principle is that you have to love a subject to paint it, loves faces. So do I. During his long life of studying faces, and for that matter, attitudes and gestures that reveal the individual, Solman has in each case found the characteristic that bespeaks the whole. And in finding that, he has found the means to make a painting an abstract entity, since portrait, still-life, cityscape, or any other image, always characterizes by means of distillation.

These portraits have the double virtue of being at once paintings and portraits thanks to Solman's thorough understanding of the nature of painting.

Much of Solman's expressive ability can be attributed to his unerring draftsmanship. A lifetime of quick sketching has endowed his hand with an agility that is dedicated to finding the essential line that will define a plane, search out the most telling profile of a form, place the form in its proper level of the imagined space, and, with intelligent economy, sum up its being. In the art of portraiture, drawing is crucial. When Solman arranges his sitter (and he always works from life) he has in mind the turn of a head, the incline of a body, the lift of a shoulder that will best describe the unique individual before him. To accomplish the whole, he must weigh, with his brush, each element. Drawing, then, is of vital significance. If he uses the flat of his brush, or merely its point, he is locating a form in space. In earlier work, his search is more evident, as his brush seeks out the nuances that define the human face. Later, the hand becomes sure, and he emphasizes the total posture of his sitter with encompassing outlines—a means of emphasis he says he learned as a youth when he studied the work of Gauguin.

I don't mean to suggest that Solman is a purely linear painter. On the contrary, he has a rich vocabulary as a "painterly" painter, using the full range of effects available in pigment and its thinners and binders. But his drawing with the brush is what distinguishes his portraits as paintings. No area of his canvas is mere filler. Each detail contributes to the portrayal of a distinctive person. Sometimes he catches his sitter with the merest incline of the head, sometimes with the lift of a hand, sometimes turned three-quarters, sometimes head-on. But always, the form he is painting—the human being—is ensconced in an active congeries of forms, each with its own significance.

Solman is alert to certain styles of gesture. After all, the Victorians affected a different posture, and the ancient Greeks certainly walked differently from us. When he undertook to portray his lower East Side neighborhood during the 1960s through its bohemian and flower-children denizens, he respected each individual, but finally, offered a telling commentary on the nature of that turbulent period. In the wonderful series of sketches from the subway, quickly recorded on his racing form (Solman, to my delight, is probably the only painter who ever earned his daily bread as a pari-mutuel employee at the race track), he captured the human comedy of New York as surely as Daumier had captured 19th-century Paris. In both his portraits of the disoriented youth of his neighborhood, and the working people on the subway, Solman exhibited a little of the ruthless precision found in the work of Egon Schiele, while in other portraits of family, friends and fellow painters, he shows feelings ranging from tenderness to profound respect.

In all his undertakings as a painter, Solman has, as Paul Klee said a painter must, always followed his own heartbeat. His work reflects an ethical position, maintained steadfastly despite the vagaries of artistic fashion, and forms an authentic entity within 20th-century American art history.

PL. 125. *Judy Prince*. 18 x 14. 1957. Collection Dr. Mrs. Sam Prince.

PL. 126. *Jane*. 20 X 12. 1953. Collection Jane Miller.

On the Artist's Portraits

BY A. L. CHANIN

In his Introduction to the 1966 volume on Joseph Solman's work, A. L. Chanin wrote: "He worked intensively between 1950–1955, using his friends as sitters. The idea of a solo exhibition devoted completely to serious portraits seemed so startling, outdated, or futile that Solman softened the blow with a droll preface to his December 1954 exhibition: 'A writer friend of mine was working away at a novel for some months when his indulgent grandmother finally asked him what he was doing alone in his room all that time. "I'm writing," he answered. "To whom?" she asked, beamingly.

"'Colleagues have asked what I've been painting these days and upon hearing "portraits" have added "commissions, I suppose." This is, of course, a commentary on the state of portraiture today, which in the main, has been left to the academic and commercial markets.

"'It was not primarily the camera that clicked away the centuries-old tradition of probing the human face in paint. Degas, Manet, van Gogh and Eakins all worked long after the advent of photography. But many of the recent art movements, with their ceaseless experimentation, have relegated subject to a secondary role or obliterated it entirely. Munch, Sickert, Vuillard, Modigliani and Kokoschka are among the exceptions who have kept the mainstream of portraiture alive. Sutherland in England has made an honest effort to return to it. I hope we may one day see it as a living force again in our country.'

"Larry Campbell, in *Art News*, wrote of Solman's portraits enthusiastically: 'It is supposed that it is impossible to be true both to sitter and to the demands of modern painting. But a reconciliation between the two can be made, and this strong exhibition shows how . . . the paint itself was applied to establish its own particular rhythms—complementing the others so that when examined under a magnifying glass every inch is transformed into little glowing abstractions [Plate oo]. Apart from his ability to get a compelling likeness . . . and the formal and human aspect of his work, it is the haunting color varying from local to atmospheric and synthetic, that makes the show memorable.'"

PL. 129. *Tar Cart*. 24 x 36. 1959. Collection Bill and Mary Louise Britten.

PL. 130. *Manhattan Bridge*. Oil on board. 24 x 30. Collection Dr. Bernhardt.

PL. 131. *Field Flowers and Regatta.* 20 X 12. 1956. Hirshhorn Museum.

PL. 132. *Dutch Model*. Oil on board. 20 x 12. 1956.

PL. 133. *Movie Theatre*. Oil on cotton. 19 x 19. Private Collection.

PL. 134. *Railroad Yard, Gloucester*. 18 x 24. 1953. H. F. Johnson Museum, Ithaca, New York.

PL. 135. *Still Life*. Oil on masonite. 14 x 18.
Collection Mr. and Mrs. Rueben Kaplan.

PL. 136. *Chair and Puppet*. Oil on masonite. 17½ x 12½.
Collection Ronni Solman.

PL. 137. *High Button Shoes*. Oil on masonite. 47 x 22½. 1956.

PL. 138. *Rosemary*. Oil on masonite. 18 x 14. 1957. Whereabouts unknown.

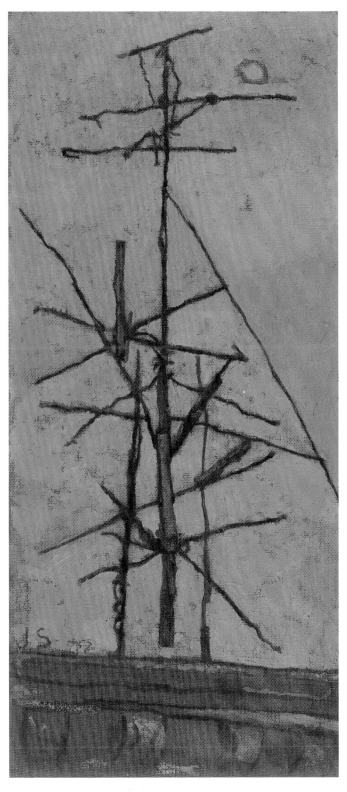

PL. 139. *Antennae*. Oil on masonite. 30 X 14. 1957.

On Solman's Work

BY JOHN SIMON

Admit it now, whom would you rather spend your life—your conversations—with: a wild untutored genius or a person of taste, wide-ranging erudition, and consummately civilized ways? The antithesis is not so much between nature and nurture as between self-absorption and universal awareness.

When I say, as I do, that Joseph Solman's art echoes most of the great art that was, I am not saying that he lacks a personal vision, that he is in any sense derivative. I am saying merely (merely?) that he seems to have seen every important artwork of the past, and un-forcedly absorbed something from each. Looking at a number of his works—or, better yet, his entire oeuvre, which, in the case of a productive artist still going strong at 85, means quite some looking—is like having a long evening's talk with an exquisitely cultivated mind. Imagine someone who in the course of swift-flying hours will quote or allude—always appropriately, easefully, and unostentatiously—to, say, the Valley of the Kings, Fermat's theorem, Alvar Aalto's buildings or furniture, the poetry of Robert Graves, the maxims of La Rochefoucauld, a bronze cardinal of Manzú, a tale by E. T.A. Hoffman, a piece of music by Samuel Barber, *greguerias* of Ramón Gómez de la serna, the love letters of Marina Tsvetaeva. And always only where it is apposite and illuminating.

So Joseph Solman's art, in all his diverse media, reflects spontaneously the entire his-tory of art—or as much as any one artist can encompass. Mention a painter you esteem, as far-fetched as you might think, and chances are I can find you someone not unlike Solman. Chirico? Certainly: the characteristic Chirico color scheme surfaces also in Solman. Soutine? But of course: humble, seemingly unlovely things transmuted into beauty. VanGogh? You betcha; the essential dignity of the lowly and mundane. Rembrandt? You've got it (or, rather, Solman has); the inexhaustible fascination of personality in a portrait. Delaunay? That, too. Games with perspective that, upon scrutiny, are not games at all, but fresh insight.

Joe has told me that all his works are based on real things. Rearranged, perhaps, rethought and transformed, but real. He is an artist for whom, as Théophile Gautier said of himself, the external world exists; he does not go around dreaming up solipsistic alternative worlds. Mention someone like Cy Twombly to Solman, and listen to what you'll get in response. All of Solman's work seems to be saying, "Anyone can paint what never was, will be, or ought to be. The trick is to paint what is there, but not slavishly. Rather, with a twinkle in your eye and heart: understanding the people and things of this world better than they understand themselves."

And now I am going to say something about Solman that, hastily, you might mistake for a platitude, so don't stop reading after the next sentence. He paints (or draws, or whatever) dreams of reality. Not dreams the way the Surrealists dreamed them up, or the Magic Real-ists exaggerated them. Dreams as they really are: reality intensified. Think about your dreams: do they contain unicorns, hob-goblins, diaphanous virgins with ankle-length tresses of pure gold? Or weird objects out of left field or even farther? Things that look like a Max Ernst, a Roberto Matta, a Pierre Soulages? They are fine painters all, but three whose dreams Solman's works do not resemble. Because dreams are more, not less, real than reality.

When you think back, then, on one of your dreams, what do you recall? A sense of strange things happening as if they were absolutely natural: intense, extraordinary, even unique. But not obviously, showily excogitated. Instead, the way a dream *does* differ from reality, by being more concentratedly, more strikingly *felt*. Look at a work such as *The Geranium Plant*, a 1975 Solman monotype, Pl. 145. A round, white garden table; three white garden chairs, asymmetrically disposed; a geranium plant on the table; a blue-green, shimmering background. There is a unifying principle: the three chairs, three red blooms, three table legs. But the threes are not aggressively thrust at you. Does it remind you of someone? Vuillard? Perhaps. Matisse? Sort of, but not really. Joseph Solman? Definitely.

Now try an earlier work, *The Broom*, Pl. 81, an oil painting of 1947. It is tremendously real, even if the lines are slightly bent out of shape, the colors somewhat more rapturous than they would seem (have you ever seen a broom with such a red in it? a dust pan with so much green?), the dialogue between warm on the left and cool on the right so heightened in eloquence? And just so that the red in the brush should not seem too studiedly solitary, there is an echo of it in the neck of a bottle on the far right. And if you look at this picture long enough, I guarantee you will discover more and more memorable things in it.

A portrait? How about *Jane*, of 1953, Pl. 126. Does the outspoken yet shapely nose, the elongated but persuasive neck, the neat though unregimented chignon suggest anyone's portraits to you? Modigliani? In a way. Carpaccio? Also. The lyrical serenity of a Gwen John? Rather. But that expression—the slightly lowered, inward, faintly melancholy gaze—*that* is something strictly between Jane and Joseph. *That* is nowhere else but here. It is life in all its humility, pridefulness, truth. How right that the painter should be called Solman: he has captured the soul of man and woman, here and everywhere he has looked. And in interiors, cityscapes, still lifes, the soul of things.

PL. 140. *Rosalind Browne*. 30 x 24. 1958. Chatham College, Pittsburgh, Pennsylvania.

PL. 141. *Jeff in Duffel Coat*. 24 x 18. 1959. Collection Lillian Shapiro.

PL. 142. *Studying the Dopesheet.*

Watercolor on newsprint. 13 X 9. 1965. Whereabouts unknown.

PL. 143. *Mother with Children.* Watercolor on newsprint.

13 X 11. 1960. Collection Ronni Solman.

PL. 144. *The Last Furlong.* 18 x 24. 1963. Private Collection.

PL. 145. *Geranium Plant*. Monotype.
10½ x 14. 1975. Collection Jan Freeman.

PL. 146. *Good Harbor Beach*. Monotype. 11 x 15. 1973. Collection Mr. and Mrs. Stan Schneider.

PL. 147. *Birds in Flight*. Monotype. 11 X 15. 1973. Collection Kit Currie.

PL. 148. *Public Theatre at Dusk*. Monotype. 15 x 11. 1983. Collection Robert and Elizabeth Bourne.

PL. 149. *Yuppie in Subway*. Watercolor on newsprint. 14 X 10. 1971.

PL. 150. *Winter Landscape*. Oil on masonite. 27 X 17. 1942.

PL. 151. *The Pianist*. Oil on board. 24 x 16. 1951.

Solman's Tracks in Time

BY JO ANN LEWIS

New York painter Joseph Solman, 76, has not had a major exhibition in Washington since his retrospective at the Phillips Collection 35 years ago. Yet his current show at Robert Brown Contemporary Art, which spans 50 years, reveals the artist's remarkable staying power. His small paintings from the '30s are as fresh as the day they were made. His recent drawings and monotypes show a vigor, authority and originality undiminished by time.

This show—which follows major exhibitions held last year at the Wichita Art Museum and in New York—begins with a few large oils, including one on loan from the National Museum of American Art. But the highlights are several small gouaches from the Depression years, when Solman—like so many other American painters—was working for the Works Progress Administration, and threading his way through the opposing camps of social realism and modern abstraction. Subscribing to neither exclusively, he evolved his own blend of the two, adding warm, expressionistic overtones.

From the start, it was the visual clutter of urban life that captivated him—especially the city streets with their jumble of signs, symbols, stoplights, streetlights, arrows, letters and painted pointing fingers. He saw them in patterns, shapes and colors, and painted them as if they were still lifes, often flattening them into dark, moody, collage-like compositions.

The results are semi-abstractions in which perspective and literal color are abandoned for the sake of all-over impact and design. Yet Solman's goals have never had anything to do with geometry, but everything to do with conveying an aura that echoed his own passionate, often playful pleasure in all he observed: a child on a tricycle, surrounded by lampposts, hydrants and signs; a pawnshop window with a lone guitar; an "Alley in Hartford," where a large painted hand points to another sign advertising chewing gum.

Today, these small paintings are filled with the warmth of remembrance, of nostalgia for bits of city life now gone—like the ice cellar with an honor-system sign-up sheet for customers. Yet, almost miraculously, none of these works has become in any way "dated"—the ultimate test of any work of art.

A fine colorist, Solman also draws supremely well, and proves it in the swift, sure outlines of the "Handicapper" and various other subway types he continues to observe (and gently caricature) during his frequent trips to Aqueduct Racetrack. He has also taken to making monotypes in recent years, using vigorous line and impressionistic color to examine new city phenomena, such as a "Motorcycle Duo," "The Pan Am Building" and "The Public Theater at Dusk."

Taken together, the show sketches out a long career of which Solman has every reason to be proud. It also underscores a major fact of today's art world: Beyond the blinding glare of the new and the trendy is a treasure-trove of *old* talent making a strong comeback. It appears to have dawned, at last, on many collectors that this is art that has already stood the acid test of time. This welcome update on Solman continues at 1005 New Hampshire Ave. NW through April 13. Hours are noon to 5 p.m. Tuesdays through Saturdays.

The Washington Post, April 4, 1985.

PL. 154. *Ignacio*. 30 x 24. 1973. Collection Dr. Milton Best.

PL. 155. *Carmen*. 30 x 20. 1962. Collection Mr. and Mrs. Al Isselbacher.

PL. 156. *Alison*. 32 x 24. 1967. Collection Mr. and Mrs. Frank Donnola.

PL. 157. *The Civil War Uniform.* 24 x 16. 1967. Collection Mr. and Mrs. Barry Gerson.

PL. 158. *Bruce and Sandra*. 72 X 52. 1970.

PL. 159. *Lynn*. 40 X 20. 1963. Collection Mr. and Mrs. Michael Goldberg.

PL. 160. *Still Life*. 24 x 18. 1968. Private Collection.

PL. 161. *John*. 24 x 18. 1969. Collection John Rushton.

PL. 162. *Dario*. 48 x 24. 1972. Rose Art Museum, Waltham, Massachusetts.

PL. 163. *Yulia*. Oil on board. 24 x 16. 1967.

PL. 164. *Chris*. 24 x 18. 1969. Collection Mr. and Mrs. Marc Weiss.

PL. 165. *East Village Couple*. 40 x 24. 1962. Private Collection.

Mining the Riches of Realism in Paint

HIGHLIGHTS 1933–93

BY NANCY STAPEN

Solman received some belated recognition in the '60s and '70s, when he was the recipient of a number of prestigious awards, a monograph was published by Crown Press and a number of retrospective exhibitions were organized in Washington and New York. Influential behind the scenes on several generations of artists, Solman sums up his aesthetic philosophy in the statement, "I have long discovered for myself that what we call the subject yields more pattern, more poetry, more drama, greater abstract design and tension than any shapes we may invent."

The Rotenburg [Gallery] show includes a broad spectrum of gouache and watercolor paintings, drawings, prints and collages. The earliest works, from the '20s and '30s, are landscapes and cityscapes, many of New York and its environs, that show Solman's essential style of expressive realism. Trees, bridges, houses and winding roads are invested with a lively, animated spirit. Although frequently dark and moody, the images have a freshness and spontaneity unusual in these difficult mediums; it is evident that Solman's eye grasps and translates the fundamentals of form with great rapidity. Yet the balanced, harmonious quality of composition and the "rightness" of form suggest years of study.

These same qualities are evident in Solman's pictures of subway riders, all painted on newspaper. His passengers are rendered with a marvelous feeling for gesture — the ability to express weight, posture and personality in a few swift strokes. It is wonderful to imagine Solman as an artist supple enough to use the models at hand, sketching away on the subway, which he once called "my favorite studio."

Given Solman's predilection for flatness and the distilled simplicity of Japanese art, it is not surprising that his most recent works are *sumi* ink sketches executed in a highly calligraphic style. There are two images of motorcycles, which although parked seemed filled with jaunty energy, plus a brush and ink depiction of objects in the artist's studio that transforms the inanimate into an image that pulsates with a near-audible heartbeat. Solman emerges as an artist whose curiosity about the natural world was matched by a thorough immersion in art's formal properties.

The Boston Globe, September 30, 1993.

PL. 166. *Art Student*. 42 x 42. 1971.

PL. 167. *Manhattan Bridge*. 14 x 17. 1941. Collection Mr. and Mrs. Carl Goldberg.

PL. 168. *Ronni*. 14 x 10. 1963. Collection Ronni Solman.

PL. 175. *Martin Dworkin*. 30 x 24. 1983.

PL. 176. *Old Parish Cemetery*. 12 x 8. 159. Private Collection.

PL. 177. *Trees, Fishkill, New York*. 20 x 12. 1938.

PL. 178. *Eve.* 48 x 34. 1968.

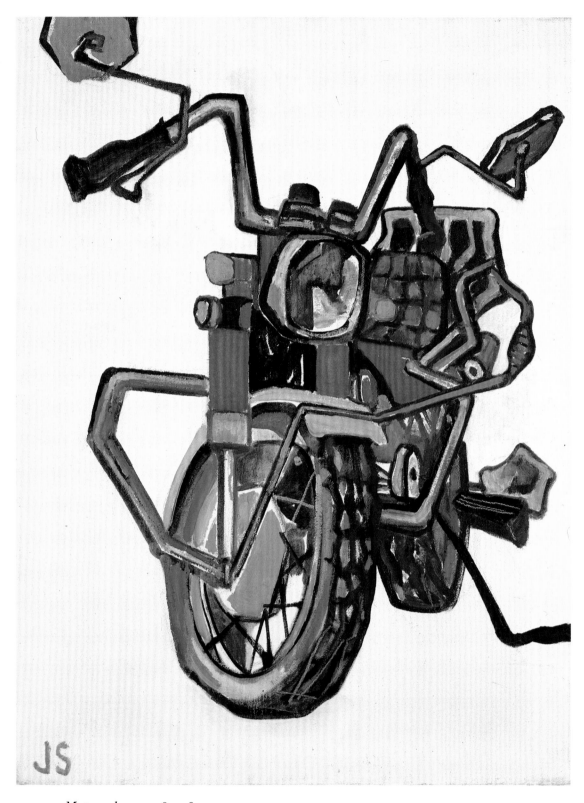

PL. 179. *Motorcyle.* 24 x 18. 1980.

PL. 180. *The Gang.* 24 x 30. 1980.

PL. 181. *Parked*. Monotype. 10 x 16. 1980. Collection British Museum.

PL. 182. *Slava*. 24 x 18. 1992. Collection Ruth Solman.

PL. 183. *Hallway*. 20 x 12. 1987. Private Collection.

PL. 184. *Hallway*. Oil on paper. 24 x 18. 1988.

PL. 185. *Golden Girl.* 24 x 16. 1979.

PL. 188. *Crumpled Paperback*. Oil on masonite. 12 x 20. Collection Mr. and Mrs. Dennis Flavin.

PL. 189. *Linda*. 24 x 18. 1988. Collection Dr. and Mrs. Michael Schlossberg.

PL. 190. *West 34th Street.* 20 X 12. 1992.

PL. 191. *Passageway*. 26 X 36. 1987–88.

PL. 192. *59th Street*. 45 x 28. 1994.

PL. 193. *Store For Rent*. 24 x 36. 1992.

PL. 194. *Abandoned Storefront*. 18 x 24. 1992.

PL. 195. *Parking Sign.* 15 x 30. 1992.

PL. 196. *St. Marks Place.* 24 X 30. 1993.

PL. 197. *Late Afternoon, West Side*. Oil on board. 12 x 20. 1990.

PL. 198. *Graffiti.* 30 x 50. 1994–95.

204

Chronology

1909. Born in Vitebsk, Russia.

1912. Emigrated to the United States.

1926. Began art studies at the National Academy of Design, New York City.

1932. Exhibited ten early gouaches (1931) at the second Washington Square outdoor show in New York.

1933. Married Ruth Romanofsky.

1934. First one-man exhibition, at the Contemporary Arts Gallery, New York City where Mark Tobey and Rothko were also introduced.

1935. Formation of the group called "The Ten" at Solman's studio which included Rothko, Adolph Gottlieb, Bolotowsky, Ben-Zion, and others.

1935–41. Worked in the easel division of the WPA Arts Project.

1937–38. Editor-in-chief *Art Front* magazine with co-editors Harold Rosenberg and Meyer Shapiro.

1938. Invited as a new member of J. B. Neumann's New Art Circle Gallery which included Max Beckmann, Rouault, Klee, Chagall and Max Weber.

1938. "Whitney Dissenters" exhibition of "The Ten" at the Mercury Gallery, New York City.

1940. Three-man show of Gromaire, Rothko, and Solman at the Neumann-Willard Gallery.

1949. Exhibition of 38 oils, spanning fifteen years of work, at the Phillips Collection, Washington, D.C.

1950. Joins ACA Gallery, New York City.

1950–54. Invited to Whitney Annuals.

1952. One of 75 American artists chosen for an important European travelling exhibition sponsored by the State Department of the United States.

1956. Takes wife, Ruth, and children, Paul and Ronni, for a first, three-month trip to Europe.

1961. National Institute of Arts and Letters award for painting.

1965. Elected president of the Federation of Modern Painters and Sculptors.

1966. Publication of book *Joseph Solman* by Crown Publishers, New York, covering work from 1929 to 1964.

1967. Elected Academician to the National Academy of Design.

1967–75. Taught art at City College of New York as part-time instructor.

1968. Purchases summer house in Gloucester, Massachusetts and concentrates on the technique and production of monotypes.

1977. Da Capo Press publishes *The Monotypes of Joseph Solman* with introduction by Una Johnson.

1983. Retrospective exhibition, *Work of the Thirties*, at both the ACA Gallery, and A. M. Adler Fine Arts, New York City.

1984. Retrospective continued at the Wichita Art Museum with a total of sixty paintings.

1985. "Joseph Solman's New York: 50 years of painting, 1934–84" at Robert Brown Contemporary Art Gallery, Washington, D.C.

1986. Exhibition *Joseph Solman: Portraits, A Fifty Year Survey*. ACA Gallery, New York City.

1988. *Paintings 1929 to 1949*. Exhibition at Judi Rotenberg Gallery, Boston, Massachusetts.

1990. Exhibition of paintings at Salander-O'Reilly Gallery, New York.

Retrospective of the 1960's East Villagers paintings at Judi Rotenberg Gallery, Boston.

Publication by Vintage Books (Random House), New York, of *Mozartiana: Two Centuries of Notes, Quotes and Anecdotes about Wolfgang Amadeus Mozart*, collected and illustrated by Joseph Solman, to coincide with the events commemorating the 200th anniversary of the composer's death in 1791.

Also published by Vintage Books for the anniversary, a 1991 wall calendar consisting of reproductions of twelve Mozart portraits from the portfolio issued by Solman in 1945.

1994. Retrospective at the Mercury Gallery, Boston, of portrait paintings made 1926–94.

Museum Collections PARTIAL LISTING

British Museum, London, England.

Butler Institute of American Art, Youngstown, Ohio.

Canton Art Institute, Canton, Ohio.

Carnegie Institute, Pittsburgh, Pennsylvania.

Corcoran Gallery, Washington, D.C.

Chatham College of Art, Pittsburgh, Pennsylvania.

Dayton Art Institute, Dayton, Ohio.

Dresden National Gallery, Dresden, Germany.

Edwin A. Ulrich Museum of Art, Wichita, Kansas.

Fogg Museum of Art, Harvard University, Cambridge, Massachusetts.

Griffiths Art Center, Canton, New York.

Herbert F. Johnson Museum of Art, Ithaca, New York.

Hirshhorn Museum, Washington, D.C.

Jewish Museum, New York City.

Museum of the City of New York.

National Academy of Design, New York City.

National Collection of American Painting, Washington, D.C.

New York Public Library.

Nevada Museum of Art, Reno, Nevada.

Oklahoma Museum of Art, Oklahoma City, Oklahoma.

The Phillips Collection, Washington, D.C.

Rose Art Museum, Brandeis University, Waltham, Massachusetts.

The Tennessee Fine Arts Center, Cheekwood, Tennessee.

University of Arizona, Tucson, Arizona.

Weatherspoon Art Museum, Greensboro, North Carolina.

Whitney Museum of American Art, New York City.

Yale University of Art, New Haven, Connecticut.

Yonkers Art Museum, Yonkers, New York.

Selected Bibliography

"Solman's New York." Illustrated. *American Arts Monthly*, Spring 1935.

Sidney Janis, preface to catalogue of 1942 exhibition of interiors, still lifes, and portraits at Bonestell Gallery, New York.

Dorothy Seckler, "Solman Paints a Picture." Illustrated. *Art News*, Summer 1951.

Suzanne Burrey, "The Growth of Conviction." Illustrated. *Arts Magazine*, October 1955.

Dorothy Seckler, "Problems of Portraiture." Illustrated. *Art in America*, Winter 1958–59.

Pop, Pop, Whence Pop. Page 8 of exhibition catalogue, Heckscher Museum, Huntington, New York, 1965.

Joseph Solman. Introduction by A. L. Chanin. 148 illustrations. Crown Publishers, New York, 1966.

Joseph Solman, "The Easel Division." Memoir in *The New Deal Arts Projects: An Anthology of Memoirs*," edited by Francis V. O'Connor. Smithsonian Institution, Washington, D.C., 1964.

The Monotypes of Joseph Solman, 41 plates in full color. Introduction by Una Johnson, curator emeritus of prints, Brooklyn Museum. Designed by Abe Lerner. Da Capo Press, New York, 1977.

Kunstlerplakate aus den U.S.A. Exhibition at the Staatliche Kunst Sammlungen, Dresden. Page 75.

Dr. Piri Halasz, *The Expressionist Vision: A Central Theme in New York in the Forties*. Catalogue and exhibition at the C. W. Post Center, Long Island University, Brookville, New York. New York State Council on the Arts, 1983–84.

Theodore F. Wolff, "The Many Masks of Modern Art." Full-page article on the retrospective exhibition, *Joseph Solman: Work of the Thirties*. *Christian Science Monitor*, Boston, May 5, 1983.

Gail Stavitsky, "Joseph Solman," full-page review of exhibition of portraits by Solman at the ACA Gallery in New York. Illustrated. *Art News*, April 1986.